YOU ARE NOT A BAD PARENT

A PEDIATRICIAN'S GUIDE TO REDUCING CONFLICT AND CONNECTING WITH YOUR TEENS

BY
ELIZABETH R. HENRY, MD

You Are Not A Bad Parent
A Pediatrician's Guide To Reducing Conflict and Connecting With Your Teens
Copyright © 2021 by Elizabeth R. Henry, MD

Book cover photo by Tinnetta Bell Photography

All rights reserved. No part of this book may be reproduced in any form without permission in writing from the author. Reviewers may quote brief passages in reviews. For permission requests, write to the author at drliz@drlizconsulting.com. www.youarenotabadparent.com

Disclaimer & FTC Notice
No part of this publication may be reproduced or transmitted in any form or by any means, mechanical, or electronic, including photocopying or recording, or by any information storage and retrieval system, or transmitted by email without permission in writing from the publisher.

While all attempts have been made to verify the information provided in this publication, neither the author nor the publisher assumes any responsibility for errors, omissions, or contrary interpretations of the subject matter herein.

This book is for educational purposes only. The views expressed are those of the author alone, and should not be taken as expert instruction or commands. The reader is responsible for his or her own actions.

Adherence to all applicable laws and regulations, including international, federal, state, provincial, and local governing professional licensing, business practices, advertising, and all other aspects of doing business in the US, Canada or any other jurisdiction is the sole responsibility of the purchaser or reader.

Neither the author nor the publisher assumes any responsibility or liability whatsoever on the behalf of the purchaser or reader of these materials.

Any perceived slight of any individual or organization is purely unintentional.

Praise For Dr. Liz's Work

"What can I say about Dr. Liz…

well she helped me get through one of the toughest years of my life. Covid hit just as my oldest daughter was diagnosed with depression and anxiety. Well as you can imagine, the isolation was difficult for everyone in my family but really tough on my oldest daughter. We were ill equipped to help our daughter and there were so little mental health resources available. My daughter's therapy was not progressing, and I truly felt helpless and alone. Not sure what to do, I turned to the one person I knew who could help. I turned to Dr. Liz. She is the perfect combination of medical and practical knowledge. She shares her experiences as a mom but also gives you real tools to help nurture your relationship with your teen. With her help, I felt empowered to take a more active role in my daughter's therapy and support her as she faces the challenges ahead.

Louise
Parent

"Dr. Liz really listened and gave me sound advice when my teenager began to experience anxiety and depression in response to the pandemic. She approached the relationship from a realistic perspective. And she gave me some tools to help both me and my son address setbacks and adversity in challenging times. She doesn't offer magic bullets, but rather pragmatic advice designed to help you understand your child's point of view. Thank you Dr. Liz!"

Stephanie T.
Parent

"Dr. Liz designed and led a successful online student empowerment workshop for USC students called "It's Your Future -- Fight On!" -- tapping into the USC motto, Fight On! The hourlong event was held at the height of anxiety during the pandemic and in the wake of widespread protests following the death of George Floyd.

Speaking openly and from the heart, Dr. Liz helped our students identify specific steps to take charge of their lives, move forward and and attain the future they want despite current circumstances. It was powerful to watch, as students accessed the tools Dr. Liz provided and let go of the fears and anxieties that were standing in their way.

We are forever grateful to Dr. Liz for her generosity and willingness to help our students and parents. Fight On, Dr. Liz!"

Rory Bennett
TV Director/Producer
USC Parent and Alumna

"Dr. Liz is a passionate leader in the industry of personal-development. Her impassioned workshop for college students helped to inspire my USC student to think about the importance of self-care in a way that really resonated. She is so relatable and her work is so needed in the lives of young people."

Dr. Isabel Springer
Therapist and Founder, LovEd

"If every physician who treats children in this world was as dynamic and dedicated as Dr. Elizabeth Henry – or "Dr. Liz," as we know her at Saint Peter's – the overall health of children everywhere would take a dramatic leap forward. Dr. Liz is the model pediatrician. I say that not only because of her doctoring skills, but because of Dr. Liz's consistent willingness to preach the mantra of improving children's health in every forum that is available to her. Dr. Liz has been a steady and forceful voice for children as a public speaker, as an expert guest on numerous radio and television shows, and in a variety of published articles in the print media. As a media professional myself, I'm always impressed by her enthusiasm and skill in advancing the cause of better health for children and teens, and their families."

Phil Hartman, VP/Chief Communications Officer
Saint Peter's Healthcare System, New Brunswick, NJ

"Dr. Liz = Pure gold! She's made for TV both in looks, knowledge, and her ability to speak in bites. Dr. Liz has great chemistry with Dr. Steve. We would welcome her back on the show. She is a Star!"

Dave Brown, Executive Producer
"Dr. Steve Show," New York, New York

In loving memory of my mother, June Lorraine Flippin
I am who I am because of her love and her listening.

ACKNOWLEDGEMENTS

I would like to thank God for giving me the courage and faith to step out of my comfort zone to make a difference for parents and youth.

I would like to extend my love and gratitude to my husband Keith, who has supported me in every endeavor I've undertaken, even if the path wasn't clear, and my daughter Lauryn for her love and inspiration.

I wish to thank Eileen Monesson for supporting me from the beginning and constantly reminding me to write a book; Melanie Gorman for rekindling my joy in writing; and Joshua Sprague for his guidance in writing, marketing, and publishing this book.

I would like to extend my profound gratitude to Deborah Chen, Cassandra Jennings, and Karen Ruffin for generously taking the time to provide me with feedback.

I would like to express my love and appreciation to all of my family and friends who continue to support me as my vision unfolds.

Your Free Gift

As a thank you for purchasing this book, I'd like to give you exclusive access to my audio training, "The Extraterrestrial Approach To Listening."

Go to www.youarenotabadparent.com to access your bonus gift.

TABLE OF CONTENTS

INTRODUCTION 1

PART 1- THE SOURCE OF CONFLICT 7
- *CHAPTER 1 - COMMUNICATION IS KEY* 9
- *CHAPTER 2 - DIFFERENT WORLDS* 13
- *CHAPTER 3 - A PARENT'S WORLD*....................................17
- *CHAPTER 4 - A TEEN'S WORLD* 25
- *CHAPTER 5 – CONFLICT* 29
- *CHAPTER 6 - PARENTAL PITFALLS* 37
- *CHAPTER 7 - SHIFTING YOUR VIEW*................................49

PART II—HOW TO REDUCE CONFLICT, STRENGTHEN YOUR CONNECTION, AND TRANSFORM YOUR RELATIONSHIP 53
- *CHAPTER 8 - DIFFERENT PERSPECTIVES*...........................55
- *CHAPTER 9 - WORDS MATTER*..59
- *CHAPTER 10 - APOLOGIES MAKE A DIFFERENCE*...............61
- *CHAPTER 11 - EXPRESSING YOUR LOVE*..........................63
- *CHAPTER 12 - LEARN HOW TO LISTEN*...........................67
- *CHAPTER 13 - BE INTERESTED AND ENGAGED* 71
- *CHAPTER 14 - ASK FOR HELP* 75
- *CHAPTER 15 - PARENTING THROUGH THE PANDEMIC*....79
- *CHAPTER 16 - SELF-CARE IS CRUCIAL* 83
- *CHAPTER 17 - PUTTING IT ALL TOGETHER* 87

THE NEXT STEP 89

ABOUT THE AUTHOR 91

APPENDIX 93

INTRODUCTION

The teenage years are trying times for parents. At one time, your children depended on you for everything. Now, they are becoming more independent, and your relationship may seem distant. They spend significantly more time in their rooms or with their friends.

I refer to adolescence as the Jekyll and Hyde phase of life. Teens are hot and cold; they're on and off. It's challenging to deal with their unpredictable moods and know-it-all attitudes. You may never be sure what to say or the best way to approach them. You hope they come to you with problems or challenges but may be finding it harder to communicate with them.

These feelings are entirely normal. I struggled with them myself raising my daughter. Even though I knew she would eventually grow into a mature adult, knowing made no difference. It's hard to let your kids go. It's difficult seeing them grow into unique individuals with different thoughts and opinions. My 23-year-old daughter still has to remind me that she is all grown up and can make her own decisions.

Dealing with the rollercoaster of emotions during the adolescent years can be frustrating, confusing, and draining, especially now during the pandemic. Work-life balance has gotten even more difficult now that your kids are remotely learning from home. Your teens may be disappointed about not seeing their friends or participating in the activities they love. You may say to yourself things like, "Why doesn't my teenager talk to me? Why don't they listen? Where did I go wrong?" These times are tough. You are certainly not alone, and you are not a bad parent if you feel this way. The road ahead may be challenging, but there are still ways to strengthen your connection with your teens and draw them closer.

Who Should Read This Book?

I wrote this book to support parents struggling to connect and communicate with their teens. It's written to empower you when you have self-doubts. It's natural for us to question our parenting ability when conflict and misunderstanding arise with our teens. Many parents second guess themselves and doubt their parenting skills when things go awry. You may feel inadequate and think you're a terrible parent. I wrote this book to encourage you and offer support and practical advice to help you through.

I hope that this book will transform your relationship with your teens. My goal is to take your connection to the next level by bridging the gap between you and your teens so you can connect and communicate with compassion and understanding.

This book provides you with tools to reduce conflict, connect with your adolescents, and navigate this tumultuous time of life. It doesn't matter what type of relationship you have now. You can improve it. Don't settle for mediocrity. You can transform a bad relationship into a good one and a great relationship into one that is extraordinary.

As you read this book, you will assess your relationship by looking at where you and your teens are now. Once you authentically look at that, you will see a whole new realm of possibilities for improving your connection with your teens.

Who am I?
I am a board-certified pediatrician, parent coach, youth advocate, and founder of Dr. Liz Consulting. I have over 20 years of experience as a trusted advisor to parents and youth.

I graduated from Princeton University and the University of Pennsylvania's Perelman School of Medicine. I completed my pediatric residency at Georgetown University Hospital in Washington, DC, then worked at the Children's Hospital of Philadelphia before joining a private practice in New Jersey.

After advising thousands of families, I realized that parents with teens needed additional support in the area of communication. Parents would often ask for strategies to steer their teens in the right direction. They were worried about their teens succumbing to peer pressure and making poor choices. They needed help in having conversations about substance abuse, social media usage, and friend groups. Many parents were concerned about their teens distancing themselves from the family, and they needed guidance on how to connect and engage with them.

I also saw an increasing number of teens with anxiety, headaches, and gastrointestinal issues caused by stress. Many of these teens didn't require therapy. They needed to learn strategies to cope and methods to discover their strengths and increase their confidence. Parents needed to know how best to support them.

Besides my traditional medical expertise, I have been trained in the areas of communication and listening. I have mastery in the areas of problem-solving, conflict resolution, and relationship building.

After spending two decades observing and talking to parents and teens, I developed a transformational template that addresses the communication gap that naturally develops as teens strive for autonomy. Since this extended beyond the scope of my practice, I created my consulting company to fully support parents and teens through coaching, workshops, and public speaking. My goal is to provide parents with a preventive approach that elevates and strengthens their relationship with their teens, ultimately creating a powerful connection.

What You're Going to Learn

There are two parts to this book. In the first part, we will focus on the source of conflict between parents and teens. We discuss why conflict arises and outline the pitfalls of parenting. These include taking things personally, thinking you're a terrible parent, being right and trying to win, handing over your emotional baggage, and thinking your teens are miniature versions of you. We end this section by looking at your approach to conflict and ways to shift your view.

In the second part of the book, we discuss methods for reducing conflict, strengthening your connection, and transforming your relationship with your teens. We begin by discussing how to recognize and acknowledge your teens' different perspectives. We then examine the significance of word choice and tone and how they profoundly impact the nature of your relationship.

You will discover how apology, acknowledgment, and unconditional love are powerful tools for keeping the connection strong between you and your teens. You will also learn how to listen effectively and understand the importance of being interested, vulnerable, and engaged. The book's final section discusses the necessity of asking for help, creating a support network, and allotting time for self-care.

This book serves as a resource to help you handle the challenges that arise during the teenage years. When things get complicated, refer to it to regain confidence in your parenting skills and to find ways to strengthen your connection with your teens. It may seem that you are saying or doing the wrong things at times, but that's normal. You're not going to be perfect, but communication is essential to connecting with your teens no matter what the situation.

PART 1 - THE SOURCE OF CONFLICT

CHAPTER 1 - COMMUNICATION IS KEY

My mother and grandmother raised me in a small New Jersey suburb outside of New York City. Computers, the internet, and cell phones hadn't been invented yet. I spoke to my friends face to face or over the phone rather than through words on a screen. I played outside on the playground until the streetlights came on and used a payphone to call my mother to pick me up from the softball field. I typed my high school and college papers on a typewriter and didn't worry about terrorist attacks, school shootings, or being bullied through a computer monitor.

As parents, we can't compare how we grew up with how our teens are growing up. Times have dramatically changed for teens. Things have gotten far more complex. They worry about how they look on social media and whether they are getting enough likes or comments on Instagram. They have the threat of school shootings, terrorist bombings, and climate change looming over their heads. If that weren't enough, now we have the pandemic! Teens have been cooped up with their parents, having limited access to their social circles. Some may be grieving the loss of family or friends and suffering from the economic impact of family members losing their jobs. They have valid concerns about their future and the future of this planet.

These issues and worries have become a teen's reality. This new reality has taken a toll. It has created stress, anxiety, misunderstanding, and conflict within the family. These obstacles impact teens' self-confidence, well-being, and ultimately their success.

Listening is key to reducing conflict and remaining engaged with your teens. You'll undoubtedly have arguments. Your adolescents may do something that goes entirely against your rules and belief systems. You most certainly will do something that embarrasses them or makes them angry. My mother did.

When I was fifteen years old, everyone wore those colorful Puma sneakers. My mother and I went to the store in a nearby town, and I tried on about four pairs. The salesclerk was a cute boy who flirted with me, and we exchanged numbers before I left. When I went home, he called the house phone, and I was excited to talk to him. Thirty minutes turned into one hour. One hour turned into ninety minutes.

At the two-hour mark, I started to hear the thumping sound my mother made when she walked using her cane. She paced back and forth in the hallway outside the door. Five minutes later, I heard a loud banging on the bedroom door. As she knocked on the door with her cane, she yelled, "Get off the phone! You've been on it way too long!"

I was mortified. I was sure the boy heard her banging and screaming. I hung up angrily, saying, "How could you do that to me? We were just talking on the phone! Why are you ruining my chances to go out with someone?" I stormed out of the room, very upset and angry.

Like most parents and teens, my mother and I saw the situation differently. My mother didn't trust the boy's intentions, while I was just happy to have his attention at all. We often fought and argued over our different perspectives. But our arguments never got in the way of our relationship. She was a social worker, a trained listener, who provided space for me to talk. Even though we disagreed at times, she fully listened to my point of view. She provided a safe space for me to express myself fully, which led to mutual trust and understanding. At the end of the day, she would always hug me to make sure I knew that I was loved.

I now have a daughter in her twenties. I know how difficult it is to bridge the communication gap between generations. I am personally familiar with the joys, pitfalls, and upsets of parenting. Sometimes, we think life will get easier as our children get older and more self-sufficient. It can be much more demanding as teens participate in more activities and develop outside interests.

Providing teens with structure and discipline while fostering their independence can also be challenging. We hope they remember the life lessons we teach them but know that we have no control over their decisions when they are with their friends. We have to worry about sexting, drugs, alcohol, cyberbullying, and the list goes on and on. Even the best kids make poor choices and get caught up in the wrong crowd. We can steer them in the right direction by listening, open communication, and understanding their world.

CHAPTER 2 - DIFFERENT WORLDS

You and your teens come from two different worlds. Your teenagers are a part of Generation Z. You may belong to Generation Y (the Millennials), Generation X, or maybe even the Baby Boomers. Let's look at the differences between these generations.

According to the Pew Research Center, Baby Boomers are 57-75 years old, were born between 1946-1964, and grew up as television programming started to expand.[1] Baby Boomers did not grow up with technology but have learned to use it to increase their productivity. They value relationships, have a strong work ethic, are goal-oriented, and tend to play by the rules.[2]

Members of Generation X are 41-56 years old and were born between 1965-1980. They learned about technology as the computer revolution took hold.[3] They were the latch key kids who grew up with MTV culture and early video games made by Atari. They didn't have cell phones or social media. Generation X is focused more on work-life balance, independence, and self-development.[4]

Millennials (Gen Y) are 25-40 years old and were born between 1981-1996. They are old enough to remember and understand the impact of 9/11. They came of age during the rapid expansion of the internet. Many entered the workforce during the 2008-2012 recession. As a result, they got a slow economic start.[5] They are confident, value achievement, and like attention; they often are characterized as the "me generation." Millennials are keenly aware of social media and technology, and they want instant gratification and recognition.[6]

Members of Generation Z are 9-24 years old and were born between 1997-2012. They have grown up with technology and are a post 9/11 generation. Either they were born after 9/11 or are too young to remember it.[7] They have matured with the threat of terrorism looming over them, and they worry about the world's general state, including climate change, school shootings, rioting, and the pandemic.

Gen Z will be one of the most educated and diverse generations. According to the Pew Research Center, most of this generation thinks that the government should do more to solve problems and that racial and ethnic diversity is good for society.[8] In my interactions with members of Gen Z, I also have noticed that they are more in touch with their feelings and are sensitive to changes in their emotional state.

Each generation has a different perspective and worldview. They have grown up in different environments and have been affected by their own distinct set of current events. Understand that you and your teens are communicating on totally different wavelengths. Some of your concerns may be the same, but many are vastly different because you have distinct priorities and goals.

Teens often focus on their wants and needs. As they become more autonomous, they try to figure out where they belong and how to fit in. They care about what others think but tend to be socially conscious and worried about the world around them. Parents are responsible for the needs of the entire family and often put the family's needs before their own. They are concerned with managing the activities of everyday living and planning for the future. Parents look at the big picture. There is nothing wrong with having these differing viewpoints, but it's important to recognize that these distinct world views can create conflict.

It's also crucial for parents to realize that the teenage brain is still growing and developing new neural connections. Your teenagers may look like full-grown adults, but the wiring in their brain doesn't fully develop until their mid-twenties.[9]

Dr. Frances E. Jensen describes these neural connections remarkably well in her book, *The Teenage Brain: A Neuroscientist's Survival Guide to Raising Adolescents and Young Adults*. She states, "In fact, the teen brain is only about 80 percent of the way to maturity. That 20 percent gap, where the wiring is thinnest, is crucial and goes a long way toward explaining why teenagers behave in such puzzling ways—their mood swings, irritability, impulsiveness, and explosiveness; their inability to focus, to follow through, and to connect with adults; and their temptations to use drugs and alcohol and to engage in other risky behavior. When we think of ourselves as civilized, intelligent adults, we really have the frontal and prefrontal parts of the cortex to thank."[10]

When my daughter Lauryn was a teen, she came home in tears and said, "Mom, I can't stand Nancy anymore! She's awful." I said, "What did she do? You're good friends." Lauryn said, "I told her I liked Tim yesterday, and today she was flirting with him." Lauryn ended up telling me the whole story and got me all riled up. I was upset with the girl too. The next day my daughter walks in as if nothing happened. She even had the nerve to be shocked that I was still mad at Nancy. My daughter said, "Oh, yeah, that. That's over. We're good now. No worries." Those mood swings were definitely hard to manage. I never knew who was going to walk through the door, Dr. Jekyll or Mr. Hyde. I had to take a deep breath and remind myself that I was dealing with the teenage brain. It's challenging and exasperating at times. Just know that their brains are still developing, and there is light at the end of the tunnel.

CHAPTER 3 - A PARENT'S WORLD

Parent Roles

As parents, you look out for your children. You are the teacher, protector, and guide. You pick them up when they fall and push them forward when they doubt themselves. We are their first teachers, showing our children how to move through the world, educating them about societal norms, and passing down our values and culture. We lay the framework and foundation for how they view life and experience it.

There are many parenting books, but they can't possibly cover all the numerous challenges that moms and dads face. Most parents use their own childhood experiences as reference guides. If they've had a good relationship with their parents, they emulate their parents' style. If they didn't have a good relationship, they often take the opposite approach. Over the years, I have witnessed many different parenting styles. Let's look at a few of the different types, keeping in mind that you may exhibit traits from each category at various times during your parenting journey.

Helicopter Parent

Two parents accompanied their 17-year-old high school junior to see me for a check-up. They carried a thick spiral-bound notebook and asked a myriad of questions about their son as if he wasn't in the room. When I answered their questions, I addressed their son directly. He was old enough to understand and take charge of his visit. It was fine for the parents to be in the room and even chime in with questions. But it was also essential for them to let their son lead the way during his appointment in preparation for doctor's visits alone.

On another occasion, a teen told me she procrastinated doing a school assignment. She would get a lower grade if she turned it in late, so her mom did the project for her. The mom's interference prevented the teen from learning how to meet deadlines and staying on task. The adolescent didn't learn anything about organization, time management, and accountability. These are all essential skills for success as an adult.

Some parents contact their child's college professors to discuss grades. Others attempt to manage everything from dorm life to meals in the college cafeteria. These are all examples of helicoptering. The parents hover and do not give their teen any space to grow and develop. They manage every aspect of their teen's life and try to fix things. Their child matures chronologically but can be socially and emotionally stunted.

Most parents want their teens to be happy. But helicopter parents think that success is the key to their children's happiness. They'll do almost anything to guarantee their teens' success. If you fall into this category, I know you have good intentions, but often you make matters worse.

Over-managing your teens is detrimental to their development. It undermines their ability to make choices and bounce back from failure. They need to understand and experience the consequences of their actions. They must learn how to manage the challenges that come their way.

When you try to fix your teens' situations or solve their problems, they don't learn how to do it themselves. If they have problems with their teachers, it's important to talk through the issues with them. They need to know how to resolve situations on their own. If their attempts to speak to their teachers don't work, then it may be time for you to step in.

It is tough to see your children go through challenges. It's difficult to know if you should intervene immediately or let them handle the situation first. There is no hard and fast rule. You have to make that call for yourself. You have to empower them with the skills to solve problems and resolve conflicts.

If they have an argument or fight with a student, talk it through with them. Help them to develop strategies to deal with it. If they have a situation with a bully and can't resolve the problem after talking to teachers, know it's time for you to intercede.

Tiger Parent

A 13-year-old girl came to my office for a check-up. She was a straight-A student and was very busy with extracurricular activities. She played the flute and participated in Model UN and the debate team. She went to Kumon after school and took on-line advanced classes on the weekend and over the summer. Her mother enrolled her in tennis because she thought it would add another dimension to her private school applications. Her mom wanted her to attend the best private school, so she was well-positioned to get into an Ivy-League college.

When I talked to the girl, I found that she loved to paint and was a talented artist. She wanted to take art classes, but her mother thought it was a waste of time and money. The girl was very anxious and did not enjoy participating in her current activities. She seemed resigned that she had no other alternatives. This was the life her mother designed for her.

The above is an example of tiger parenting. You most commonly hear about tiger moms, but there are tiger dads too. Amy Chua first coined the term in her book, *Battle Hymn of the Tiger Mother*. In this book, she described this type of parenting in detail.

Although it has been primarily associated with Asian families, tiger parenting can be found in families from different ethnicities and backgrounds. Tiger parents put extreme pressure on their teens to succeed. They enroll them in outside learning centers so they can advance quickly in school. They pressure them to participate in activities that look good on their transcript, regardless of their interests. These parents are very forceful and pushy and don't give their teens any space. [11]

In my office, teens of tiger parents have told me that if they fall short of a goal, perhaps getting a B rather than an A, their parents make them feel guilty. This is detrimental to their self-esteem. They often feel stressed and anxious trying to meet their parents' expectations. These adolescents usually do everything they can to please their parents to gain praise and acceptance. However, sometimes they rebel, leading to severe conflict in the household.

In 2010, there was a highly publicized case in which a young adult, Jennifer Pan, created an elaborate web of deception to maintain the image that she was the perfect child. Her parents put intense pressure on her to succeed and used the tiger parenting style. Jennifer forged report cards, scholarship letters, and university transcripts to make her parents believe that she was a straight-A student who went to college. In reality, she failed calculus and never received her high school diploma. Jennifer had scars on her arms from cutting, which revealed that she had emotional issues. She eventually went to extreme measures to escape her parents' control by hiring hitmen to murder them. They killed her mother and injured her dad, and the justice system sent her to prison for murder.[12]

Jennifer Pan was emotionally unstable and took horrific measures to end her relationship with her parents permanently. When she initially failed to meet her parents' expectations, she lied. When her lies fell apart, she tried to end their control over her by murdering them. Undoubtedly, this is an extreme example, but pressure, self-doubt, and inner turmoil in the absence of authentic communication can be a recipe for disaster. That's why it's essential to recognize your parenting style and be aware of its impact on your teens.

The Lenient Parent

During an office visit, a teenage boy told me that he didn't have a curfew. His parents thought he needed his independence and were giving him space. When I talked to the teen further, he felt that his parents were indifferent. Since all his friends had a curfew, he believed they didn't care.

Teens need and want autonomy. Yet, it's still essential to provide them with discipline and structure. They will always give you a hard time about the rules you set. They may say, "I'm grown. I'm not a baby anymore" or "My friend's parents don't do that. Why do I need all those rules?" It's as if they are reading lines from the same script.

Despite what they say, structure, rules, and consistency are important to them. They notice when they're not there. Teens realize that parents are supposed to be embarrassing and annoying. They thrive on talking to each other about how irritating you are. The more you bother them, the more they know that you care. So, make sure you don't let your guard down. Continue to lay the groundwork, give direction, and provide order no matter what they say.

Some parents let their teens handle everything themselves. They do this to teach them how to be independent and manage situations, but teens cannot deal with all problems. An uncaring teacher or school administrator may ignore their complaints. You may need to intervene in some cases. There are times when you have to speak up and take action for what's right for your teens.

The Friend
Being a friend to your teens is very tricky. You can be their friend, but only if you can switch to parent mode at any given moment. My mother and I were best friends. I talked to her just about every day until she passed away when she was 88. Although my mother and I were close, she was not opposed to disciplining me when I did something wrong. She would not hesitate to pull the "mom" card at any moment when needed.

My daughter and I are also close friends, and we talk almost daily as well. When my daughter crosses the line, I have no problem changing my tone and shifting to "Mom" mode. I won't hesitate to tell her when she goes too far and needs to correct her speech and actions.

You can be very close with your teenagers, but you have to remember that your teens will have many friends but only one set of parents. Your job is to provide guidance and direction, not to be liked. I've witnessed some teens disrespecting their parents without any significant correction at all. Their parents try to negotiate with them by saying things like, "Please calm down. We are in the doctor's office. I don't like that kind of language." Their attempt at reprimanding is unsuccessful. It's delivered more as a plea rather than as a demand.

You are not always going to be their friend. They are not always going to see you as that cool parent. Teens need to be told what to do at times. To effectively direct them through challenges, you need a balanced perspective. It's important to have a general understanding of their worldview to do this.

CHAPTER 4 - A TEEN'S WORLD

Teens have a lot to deal with when it comes to technology and social media. Technology is advancing at an exponential rate. New social media platforms and forms of communication are constantly being created. Now cell phones and other electronic devices are moving to 5G. Our phones and computers are being upgraded almost every year. The graphics for gaming systems improve with each version. Virtual reality is becoming more advanced as we speak.

Your teens grew up with technology. This is their life. This is how they connect, communicate, and function in the world. They are always "on," reachable, rarely unplugged. They can be bullied at home through computer screens without you even knowing it. They can connect and chat with strangers throughout the world.

Often you have no idea what they have seen or heard through their devices. They have access to information, exposing them to subject matter that may be difficult to process and not be age-appropriate. They see videos displaying violence, police brutality, racial unrest, nudity, and sexual content. Monitoring their devices 24 hours a day is not possible. Parental controls are available, but teens are brilliant. I guarantee that even the least tech-savvy teen will find a way to bypass them.

When my daughter was in middle school, I checked her grades by logging into the school's parent site. I typed in the password multiple times, but the system locked me out. The password was incorrect. I shouted upstairs, "Lauryn, what's the password for Genesis?" She answers, "It's the one we always use." I respond, "That's the one I've been putting in!" I subsequently called the school's computer help desk and said, "Something is wrong with your system. I keep typing in my password, but it locked me out." The help desk lady responded, "Oh, somebody changed that password yesterday." I stated, "Yesterday? Okay. Thank you." I hung up the phone and screamed upstairs, "LAURYN!!!"

Lauryn explained that she had gotten a zero for not handing in an assignment. She was attempting to hand in her work for partial credit and changed the password to stall for time. I grounded her for that act of deception, and she never did that again. But it showed me how my teen could manipulate technology to her advantage. Teens are a lot more tech-savvy because technology is all they know.

Teens have many other concerns growing up in today's world. Some kids are anxious about the possibility of being involved in a school shooting. Imagine going to school and being afraid that you, your friends, and your teachers may get hurt or killed!

You probably weren't concerned about those things growing up. Some of you may have gone through air raid drills or fire drills, but not school shooter drills. You did not have to see and hear the sobs and screams of parents and children as you watched the news. You didn't watch videos of police swat teams escorting school kids to safety. This is a new reality that your teens are facing.

If you are a person of color, your teens have to handle the additional stress of dealing with race. They worry about how other people perceive them. They are concerned about the stereotypes they face when they walk into a room or ride their bike in their neighborhood. In the media, they see people that look like them needlessly killed on the street over and over again. These teens view angry citizens protesting and rioting and may personally know victims of racial profiling and violence. They wonder if those situations will happen to them. They feel the divisiveness rising around them like a thick cloud and wonder what their future will hold.

Your teens also notice the physical changes that have occurred on this planet. They see the increased number of hurricanes and wildfires. They experience unusually mild winters and sweltering summers. They hear about the ice caps melting, the seas rising, and the beaches eroding. They realize the planet is changing and not for the better.

Most recently, your children have had to deal with the impact of the pandemic. They were forced to learn remotely. They no longer had daily physical contact with their teachers and friends. They stopped participating in extracurricular activities they loved so much. Athletes no longer played their sport. Dancers and actors no longer performed on stage. Most seniors did not have in-person graduations, and many did not have proms.

Everything teens knew and loved stopped. They had to wear masks and stand 6 feet away from people. They were socially isolated inside their homes. Some had to deal with the death of a family member, friend, or even a teacher. They may have had parents who lost their jobs and are struggling to make ends meet. We have yet to know the ramifications of the pandemic on this generation. We need to be ready to deal with the educational, social, and emotional consequences of virtual learning, social isolation, and economic insecurity.

Now more than ever, conflict is bound to increase in the home. Everyone is under intense pressure and stress. Parents and teens have different perspectives. They clash as they try to manage their frustrations, disappointments, sadness, and worry.

CHAPTER 5 – CONFLICT

What is Conflict? Conflict is simply a disagreement or argument that arises as a result of differences of thought and opinion. It happens when people disagree over ideas, values, or desires. It stems from believing that you're right and the other person is wrong. Conflict can occur over something big or small but grows when ignored.

I have witnessed various forms of conflict between teens and parents. In one instance, a sixteen-year-old girl told her parents that she was going to a friend's house every day after school. Instead, she went to her boyfriend's house. Neither of his parents was home. You can imagine what happened when the girl's father found out the truth. He went ballistic, yelling and screaming at both the girl and her boyfriend.

Being a teen, she was embarrassed and angry that her father made such a scene. She was also upset that her mother stood by and did nothing to ease the situation. Her relationship with both parents became strained. They couldn't talk to each other without their emotions getting in the way. The situation became contentious and emotional. They slammed doors and constantly yelled at each other.

The teen attempted to run away several times. No one was willing to listen to anything anyone else had to say.

In another instance, a mother was worried about her teenage son. He had trouble waking up in the morning. She spent at least 15 to 20 minutes trying to get him out of bed and frequently drove him to school because he was late. She thought there might be something physically wrong with him. It turned out that he spent countless hours playing video games in his room late at night. He was tired because he didn't get enough sleep.

She was also concerned because he secluded himself in his room most of the day after school. She felt distanced from him and did not know how to connect. He isolated himself from being with the family a lot of the time. He preferred to play games with his friends on-line.

In talking further with the teen, he was anxious about school. He was tired of his mom pressuring him about everything. She bothered him about grades, college, and being involved in activities. He just needed space. The more she nagged him, the more he retreated into his room and disconnected from the family.

Some people choose to run towards conflict, but this young man tried to retreat from it. In doing so, he created ongoing worry, upset, and distance in his relationship with his parents. There was also an increasing number of disagreements.

You may not be in the same circumstances as the parents in the above examples. Yet, I guarantee that you will have emotionally charged encounters with your teens. You will either quarrel head to head or withdraw and disengage. It will all depend upon how you both react to strife.

Your teens will test your boundaries and be rebellious at times. Teens start to look for ways to gain more independence and separate from their parents. Conflict is bound to happen, and if left unchecked, it can create irreparable harm.

Your Personal Approach to Conflict

To deal with disputes, you must first understand how you relate to strife. You may not have liked growing up in a family that argued a lot. Now, you may avoid confrontations at all costs. You do everything possible to prevent a heated exchange. You may leave the room or stop communicating altogether.

Maybe you've modeled your response after a parent who was quick-tempered. At the slight hint of a disagreement, you begin to fume, your muscles tighten, and your jaws clench. You're ready to pounce in a verbal attack, which can be more devastating than a physical altercation.

Both of these are unproductive ways of managing disputes. Avoiding the situation doesn't resolve the issue. Reacting makes things worse.

How do you handle conflict? Do you run towards it or away from it? What are your triggers?

You may be triggered by an underlying need to defend your views and ideas from being attacked. Your reaction may not be based on the situation. It may spring from a feeling of being disrespected, made wrong, or not being good enough.

To interrupt your triggers, be aware of your feelings in a particular circumstance. Ask yourself why you are feeling that way. Becoming aware allows you to be present in the situation. You no longer react from a trigger that comes from the past. Being present moment by moment is crucial to connecting with your teens.

Cost of Conflict

Relationships

We respond to conflicts from our own points of view and experiences. We often have strong emotions surrounding the issue at hand. These feelings can lead to explosive and hurtful reactions. They can also lead to avoidance, withdrawal, and an unwillingness to compromise.

The emotions can envelop you and your entire surroundings, and you can't see anything clearly. You may soon find that you and your spouse are arguing about situations involving your teens. You may be taking out your frustration on other family members, which jeopardizes those relationships as well.

That's why it's important to recognize strife when it occurs and use the strategies laid out in this book to help you deal with it effectively. Choosing not to resolve conflict with your teens will harm your relationship by creating distance, anger, resentment, and stress.

Well-being

Conflict negatively affects your well-being by causing stress and worry. These feelings can trigger the release of stress hormones which activate receptors on various organ systems.

Stress causes a series of reactions that begin in the brain. The eyes and ears send stressful information to the part of the brain called the amygdala. This area processes emotions, including fear. The amygdala sends the alarm signal to a command center called the hypothalamus, which in turn uses the nervous system to transmit it to the rest of the body. Next, your adrenal glands release epinephrine (adrenaline) and norepinephrine (noradrenaline) into the bloodstream, and your body reacts with a response known as "fight or flight." It gets a burst of energy that allows you to fight off the danger or flee from it.[13] This biochemical response is a defense mechanism created as a survival instinct during the early stages of human existence. However, it can be triggered any time you feel threatened physically or emotionally, including during disagreements with your teens.

Have your teens ever said or done something that made you clench your teeth or the hairs on the back of your neck or arms stand at attention? Have you ever felt like one of those cartoon characters who was about to blow their top? If you answered yes to those questions, then you experienced the fight or flight sensations.

Your heart rate, blood pressure, and respiratory rate increase. Your heart pumps blood to vital organs. Your small airways in your lungs get larger so you can take in more oxygen. The increased oxygen that goes to the brain causes you to be more alert. Glucose (blood sugar) and fats are released into the bloodstream from storage sites to supply energy to other parts of the body.[14]

These physiological changes cause you and your teens to be more alert and on edge. Your hearts race, and your blood pressures rise. You are ready to react and respond quickly as your disagreements escalate. You're now in fight or flight mode and prepared to defend your positions.

It's essential to find ways to reduce conflict with your teens because long-term stress can cause chronic changes in the body. If acute stress continues, the adrenal gland releases cortisol to maintain the heightened state.[15] Prolonged exposure to hormones, like cortisol, increases inflammatory responses. It can lead to hypertension, heart attacks, and stroke. Stress hormones can also communicate with receptors in the gut and cause pain, bloating, and other intestinal issues.[16] Chronic stress can lead to headaches, weight gain, and sleep problems. It can also cause memory and concentration impairment, anxiety, and depression.[17] It's crucial to learn ways to minimize conflict and manage stress to optimize both you and your teens' physical and emotional health.

Jane Okondo, a somatic movement specialist from the UK, has helpful tips for recognizing and interrupting this reactionary response. When you notice you are getting upset, you can refer to her tips below to keep your cool and thoughtfully respond to the situation rather than react to it.

1. Make a fist and open and close your hands, stretching your palms and fingers to increase the blood flow.

2. Twist your body to create mobility in your spinal area. This movement stimulates the diaphragm, a muscle associated with breathing. If your muscles feel tight, this exercise tends to open up and wake up your breathing.

3. Count your breaths. Count to three as you inhale and count to four or five as you exhale. Breathe in through your nose and

breathe out through your mouth or nose. You can extend the count to four as you inhale and count to five or six as you exhale. The goal is to make your exhalations longer. Your breathing is unique to you. When you slow your breath, it automatically begins to calm you.

4. Stand up. Bend your knees to rotate your spine. Move your whole body by bending or wiggling. When you move, you move the energy that builds up in your body during times of stress.

You can do the first three exercises without anyone noticing. If you need to calm down, walk out of the room and do the fourth exercise. After you have taken this time to pause, you should be ready to speak. Getting the body moving allows you to center yourself.[18]

Finances

Conflict with your teens can impact you financially as well. Worrying about your teens and dwelling on past arguments can cause a loss of productivity at work. You might have to pay for tutoring or summer school if your teens rebel by not doing their schoolwork. You might lose money if they quit an activity you pressured them to join. If they start acting out by fighting or using drugs, you may have legal fees for attorneys. You also may have to spend money on therapists and other resources to help deal with the situation.

Conflict can damage your relationship with your teens. You can't escape conflict, so it's best to know how to deal with it in a healthy way. You can reduce the number of disagreements by avoiding certain parental pitfalls.

CHAPTER 6 - PARENTAL PITFALLS

Taking Things Personally
When your teens lash out, it's frequently not about you. They are dealing with a lot of things they may not even share with you. They may be worrying about how they look on social media or what someone said in a comment on their most recent post. They may be thinking about not being invited to a party or about their grades in school. They have many things on their minds, and unfortunately, they may take their frustrations out on you.

No matter what we know and how much experience we have, our teens think they know more. When you talk to them, you're going to feel completely inadequate at times. Their sarcasm, harsh comments, and rolling of their eyes may cause you to doubt your parenting skills.

Although I am a pediatrician with years of experience, my daughter doesn't usually take my advice. My 20 years in practice don't count in her book. Whatever I say doesn't matter because what does mom know? I usually end up saying, "Go ask your doctor." So, keep this in mind when you interact with your kids, and don't take it personally.

My mother didn't have the money to buy a car until I was a sophomore in high school, so sometimes we took a taxicab to get to my softball games at the other end of town. I would ask her to drop me off two blocks away because I was embarrassed about not having a car. I am not sure how she felt about my request because I never asked. She may have felt bad about not being in a position to buy a car. But when I look back, my request had nothing to do with her as a person. It had everything to do with me fitting in with my peers. I was only concerned about myself at the time.

The desire to be admired and liked is a natural human trait. If your teens don't enjoy your music, fashion sense, hobbies, or traditions, don't take it to heart. They are not rejecting you as an individual or as a parent. They have different personalities and interests.

I remember being very excited to show my daughter a new sweater I bought from the store and was disappointed when she said, "You like that? Well, I would have told you not to buy that." I wanted her to share in my happiness over finding such a wonderful item. Her reaction was the opposite of what I expected. I responded by saying, "I like it, so that's what matters." I quickly ended the conversation and walked away. Looking back, I realized that I shut down the conversation with a terse comment and somewhat angry tone to hide my feelings of disappointment. I wanted my daughter to like what I liked, and when she didn't, I took myself out of the conversation.

Your teens are not going to like everything you like. They may dislike a majority of your interests because they have different passions. Just remind yourself that it's okay. They are their own person, and their diverse opinions mean nothing about you or how you parent. Embrace their differences and help to foster them.

Thinking You're a Bad Parent (Bad Parent Syndrome)

It's normal to question your parenting skills, especially when your teens' actions differ from your views and expectations. When teens break the rules, it's natural for parents automatically to think that something is wrong. You may start saying to yourself, "What's wrong with them? They know better. Where did I go wrong as a parent?" Your mind may spiral out of control, filled with questions, blame, self-doubt, and guilt. Often you fall into the trap of viewing their mistakes as a reflection of your parenting skills. You are angry that they disobeyed you, but underneath that anger, you may be concerned that people will think you're a terrible parent.

No one wants to be seen as a lousy parent. Even the worst parent gets offended when you criticize their child-rearing skills. It's human nature to want to look good and avoid looking bad. Although some parents know they aren't living up to their roles, they don't want anyone else pointing it out to them.

Your teens likely will do something foolish. That is the nature of being an adolescent. All you can do is lay the framework for your teens' development and hope they make the right choices. Stay away from labels and broad generalizations. When your teens make a mistake, there isn't anything necessarily wrong with them. They made a poor choice at that moment. You are not a bad parent, and they are not bad kids.

Here are three tips on how to effectively communicate with your teens when they make mistakes:

1. **Discuss what happened or what is currently happening, sticking to the facts.**
   When your teens make a mistake, look at what happened versus what's wrong. As soon as you think something is wrong,

you get bogged down in your opinions and feelings. You're upset, worried, or concerned. Your thoughts and feelings are valid, but your emotions cloud the situation. You worry about what other people think and how it makes you look, which does nothing to help the problem at hand. It only increases anxiety and conflict. You can reduce your emotional reactions by sticking to the facts around the situation. If you ask them what they were thinking, you probably won't get a satisfactory answer. They often don't even know what they were thinking. Remember, their frontal cortex is not fully developed.

2. **Discuss what could have been done differently to shift the outcome.**
   Take a moment to sit down with your teens and discuss different approaches to the situation. What could they have done differently? What was missing in their thought process that would have changed the outcome? What structures can they put in place so it won't happen again?

   You have an opportunity to be open, honest, and have a two-way conversation with your teens. It's best to avoid lecturing them about how they should have handled the situation. Lecturing makes no difference. Your teens will tune you out and most likely won't do what you want them to do. When you help them think through different scenarios, you teach them how to make positive choices and avoid certain outcomes.

3. **Jointly create a plan to avoid repeating the same mistake.**
   When your teens develop a plan, they are more likely to follow it because it's their plan, not yours. After your teens discuss the different choices they could have made, help them create

strategies to avoid being in that same situation again. Be interested in what they have to say. Let them know that you are listening. Give them feedback but also remember to enforce your consequences for breaking the rules. They have to learn that their actions have ramifications.

I know some of you may be rolling your eyes as you read this. You may be thinking, "I am not about to sit down and have a calm conversation with my daughter after she broke my rules and did something foolish. That may work for some parents, but I'm not doing that."

I hear you. At times, I flew off the handle when my daughter blatantly ignored the rules. None of us is perfect, and we all have different thresholds for displaying our emotions. However, yelling and dramatic emotional outbursts do more harm than good when there is no space to have a peaceful dialogue about the situation. You want your teens to know that they can come to you with any problem. Your teens need to know that there will be consequences for their actions, but you love them no matter what mistakes they have made.

Let me give you two examples of how you can put these three tips into practice.

Example 1

Let's say your teenage son does not complete many of his assignments. You might start off thinking, "What's wrong with him? How could he do this? His GPA is going to drop. Something is not right. Am I doing something wrong?"

This thinking causes you to think in terms of right, wrong, good, and bad. It prevents you from thinking clearly. When you talk to your son, he can sense that you are making him wrong, and he automatically gets defensive. There is no room to have an open conversation, and most likely, things erupt into an argument.

You can react calmly by approaching the situation by using my three tips. First, what's happening? Your son is not handing in all of his assignments, and it's bringing his grade down. Plain and simple.

Now, your job is to sit down with him and figure out how to shift the outcome. What could he do differently? The key is to work together to develop a plan.

If he forgets to write down his homework on his electronic device, you may both decide that he should write his assignments down in his notebook. If he tells you that he doesn't get along with his teacher, you can further discuss and develop strategies to address that.

Once you figure out how to shift the outcome, you can put structures in place to take action. You might help your son create a planning system that works for him or develop a partnership with his teacher. Perhaps your son would benefit by having a mentor that can provide additional support. It's essential to stick to the facts surrounding the situation and avoid reacting or responding based on your feelings.

Example 2

Suppose a teacher catches your daughter vaping in the bathroom at school. What happened? She was vaping. You don't allow her to vape, and it's against the school rules.

What can be done differently to shift the outcome? Perhaps she needs more supervision and guidance at home. Maybe she needs more attention. You might want to sit down and have an open conversation with her about it.

The next step is to come up with a plan of action. Besides disciplining your daughter for breaking the rules, you may decide to provide additional structures at home, get to know her friends, or spend more quality time with her. It's up to you to take a look and together come up with an action plan.

Being Right and Trying to Win

Misunderstandings often arise because both sides want to be correct. They occur when both parents and teens are unwilling to consider that they may be wrong. Right and wrong are usually associated with good and bad. If you are right, you tend to pat yourself on the back and feel good about yourself. If you are wrong, you often feel bad about yourself. Nobody, not even your teen wants to feel bad, so you both dig your heels in to prove your point. When this happens, you are unwilling to consider the other's point of view.

Parents and teens often argue to win. But your relationship with your teen is not a battle to win. Your relationship is something that should be nurtured, honored, and valued. And yes, it's hard. It's tricky. There are tears, mishaps, and disappointments. But your relationship will be stronger if you open up and talk to each other. You can resolve almost anything with communication.

Handing over Your Emotional Baggage

Your story is not their story. You may have had disappointments, failed relationships, and other misfortunes. You certainly don't want any of these things to happen to your children. It's natural to try to protect them, but your emotional baggage is not theirs. What happened in your past is not destined to happen in their future.

A teen came for an office visit and was upset because his father would not let him get a job after school. The boy did well in school but wanted to have a part-time job like many of his friends. He had no idea why his father was furious about the concept of him working after school. Talking about this issue created discord between them.

After talking to the father alone, the source of the conflict became apparent. The dad told me that he grew up in poverty and had to work several jobs after school to help his family. As a teen, he vowed that he would always support his family when he grew up and that his kids would never need to work while in school.

After speaking with me, the father realized that he associated having an afterschool job with being poor. Talking about the subject with his son triggered his fight or flight response and threw him into a frenzy. He felt his son's request to look for a job implied that he couldn't take care of his family, which was far from the truth. His son merely wanted to be like his friends, thought it would be fun, and wanted to earn his own spending money.

So how do you prevent yourself from handing over your emotional baggage? First, you must stop and ask yourself why the two of you are at odds. Are you worried that your teen is doing something dangerous? Are you trying to prevent your son from repeating your same mistakes? Are you concerned that a situation that happened to you will happen to your daughter? It's important to step back for a moment before the disagreement escalates and you both say and do things you regret.

Just because you had a bad experience in the school play doesn't mean your son will. If he is interested in the theater, encourage him to audition and create his own memories.

Don't prevent your son from trying out for the football team just because football players in high school bullied you. Playing a sport may do wonders for his confidence.

Your awful dating experience in high school doesn't mean that you should keep your daughter from dating. Her encounters may be different from yours.

It's important to have authentic conversations about your genuine concerns. What happened to you in the past will not necessarily occur for your adolescents. You can use your experiences as springboards to have discussions about your lives. Your teens will have plenty of their own emotional baggage. The best thing you can do is help them process theirs and avoid unintentionally handing them your own.

Thinking They're Miniature Versions of You

Keep in mind that your teens are not "mini-me's." My daughter Lauryn and I are quite different. I was a very studious girl growing up and would strive to get straight A's. I loved science and math and was okay in art but not great. My daughter was a good student but didn't care about getting A's, especially if she didn't like the class. If she happened to get a "C," her attitude was "oh well." We clashed for years on that subject but trying to force her to do the work only caused more arguments and stress.

She was incredibly talented in the arts. She started "writing books" when she was about five years old. She would make up stories, write them down on paper, and staple the pieces of paper together. When she was in the fifth grade, I gave her my old computer. She would stay up for hours learning how to edit various cartoon clips and dub in the music. My husband and I were shocked when we discovered she could sing. We almost fell over when she belted out a song in the school talent show.

It took me a while, but I finally accepted that Lauryn was gifted in the arts, not science. She was passionate about the arts. That was her sweet spot. When I finally understood and accepted this, my tension and stress markedly decreased. I began to realize that my goal as a parent was to help her develop these gifts. I became more interested in her talents and natural abilities. Our relationship grew, and we became closer.

Your children have their own identities, personalities, and talents. They are separate individuals and are not the same as you. You may be a type-A personality, and they may be type-B. You may be a scientist, and they may be an artist. You may be an athlete, and they may be a musician. They may not think like you, learn like you, or do the things that you do. Let them be their own person. Your job as a parent is to guide and nurture them to use their talent to make their mark and contribution.

I am not advocating that you accept mediocrity or low performance. Just recognize that even if you both have similar interests, your children are different. They are not miniature versions of you.

You may wonder why your teens seem unhappy, unfulfilled, and rebellious. Check in with yourself. Maybe they're not expressing themselves fully. Are they using their talents? Are they tapping into their gifts? Perhaps they are trying to conform to your desires and not their own. You can reduce conflict and strengthen your relationship with your teens by avoiding this pitfall.

CHAPTER 7 - SHIFTING YOUR VIEW

One of my favorite quotes is from John A. Taylor's "Notes from an Unhurried Journey." He states:

> *"When we adults think of children there is a simple truth that we ignore: childhood is not preparation for life; childhood is life. A child isn't getting ready to live; a child is living. No child will miss the zest and joy of living unless these are denied by adults who have convinced themselves that childhood is a period of preparation. How much heartache we would save ourselves if we would recognize children as partners with adults in the process of living, rather than always viewing them as apprentices. How much we could teach each other; we have the experience and they have the freshness. How full both our lives could be."*[19]

This quote is a reminder to be present to your teenagers' everyday moments. We often get caught up in preparing kids for adulthood. In doing so, we forget that they are living their life right now. We can all learn from each other. It's not a one-way street. We instill our values and philosophies in our children. We try to teach them right from wrong and the ins and outs of life, but they can teach us, too. They can teach us about social media and technology. They can teach us how to look at life from a young and fresh point of view. We can listen and appreciate their concern for our planet's future. They have something to say and should be heard and acknowledged for their point of view.

Now I can hear some of you saying, "That may be all well and good, but teens need to be told and shown what to do." I agree that teens need boundaries and discipline, but you must go beyond merely telling them what to do. Their inexperience doesn't mean their thoughts aren't valuable or that you can't consider their perspective.

Teens can add something fresh to an idea. They may add creativity to a project or technology to a platform. They may be able to help advance your marketing idea by bringing a youthful energy to it. They can assist you in serving others by volunteering. They can help with your outreach to the younger generation. They can aid in environmental cleanup and recycling. They can provide ideas on school safety. Don't discount them.

My daughter Lauryn summed it up best on my podcast when she said, "In terms of learning to love your kid and accept your kid, it does not start in the future. And it doesn't start when they go to college. And it doesn't start when they become a doctor. And it doesn't start when they have a family and they settle down. It starts literally right now. And that's what it's about. I think, right now, parents need to learn how to be more present with the current being of their child because... we're not guaranteed tomorrow."[20]

Value and acknowledge your teenagers. By embracing them, you can connect in ways you never imagined, especially while you are home during this pandemic. Yes, you will have conflicts, but you can reduce the number of disagreements. You can get through the teenage years with your relationship intact. The key is in your listening.

You can receive step-by-step guidance for implementing the strategies you've read so far by registering for my *21 Day Boost Your Connection with Your Teen E-mail Challenge Course* at wwwboostyourconnectionwithyourteen.com.

PART II—HOW TO REDUCE CONFLICT, STRENGTHEN YOUR CONNECTION, AND TRANSFORM YOUR RELATIONSHIP

CHAPTER 8 - DIFFERENT PERSPECTIVES

To resolve conflict, you have to be willing to consider the other person's point of view. Look at the picture below. What do you see?

What you see depends on your perspective. Do you see a vase, or do you see two faces looking at each other?

Both answers are correct. If you focus on the white part of the image, you will see a vase. If you concentrate on the black parts, you will see the profile of two faces. Your view depends on your perspective. Once you're made aware of the different perspectives, you can see that both are valid.

The same holds true in your interactions with your teens. Your view as a parent is shaped by your experiences and desire to teach, protect, and guide them. Your children's view is molded by their experiences. Their outlook stems from their desire for autonomy, adventure, fun, and exploration.

Initially, you might not be able to see the other point of view. Even when you see it, you might disagree with it, and that's okay. We are all entitled to have different viewpoints. The disconnection occurs when we aren't willing to listen to our adolescents' concerns. It happens when we invalidate them with "yeah, but..."

"Yeah, but..." is a phrase that minimizes what a teen is saying. Let's say your son expresses disappointment about a grade on a test. If you respond by saying, "Yeah, but perhaps you didn't study hard enough," then you are minimizing his concern. Taking this approach discounts your teen's perspective.

A better response would be to say, "I'm sorry you didn't get the grade that you wanted. I know you're disappointed. Do you want to talk more about it?" Now, you are acknowledging your son's feelings. He knows you are listening and understand his concern. It leaves an opening for ongoing conversation and future discussions about preparing for the next test.

It's essential to listen and acknowledge that we hear what our teens are saying so they continue to communicate with us. We can agree to disagree without invalidating their thoughts. Everyone has a right to their opinions and feelings. We are not necessarily going to convince each other to adopt the other viewpoint. But it's important to pay attention to what our teens are telling us.

CHAPTER 9 - WORDS MATTER

Sometimes words are exchanged in an argument, and it's difficult to forgive or forget. What we say makes a huge difference. It determines how our teens respond to us. Calling them names like lazy, stupid, clumsy, or awkward creates a label they internalize. They think that's who they are when it's not. Their future actions tend to fall in line with this label. They may not try to be or do anything outside of that label because, for them, that's who they are.

A mother, for example, may have had a bad day at work and comes home to find out that her son didn't do his chores. Of course, that's upsetting and should be addressed. But in this instance, she gets furious and starts yelling at her son for ignoring his chores. She not only yells, but she says in anger, "I can't believe you did this again. You're so lazy." Her reaction is way out of proportion to her son's inaction. The mom is actually reacting to the situation at work, but her son gets the brunt of it.

Words are powerful. Teens are very good at having internal dialogues with themselves. And that inner voice is usually negative and disempowering, and they analyze everything.

In the above example, the boy may think, "Why did my mom say that? She's really angry. Was it that big of a deal? She always calls me lazy. Maybe I am lazy." If he starts to believe that, he may not be as diligent in turning in assignments, doing chores, or completing other tasks. He internalizes the label of being lazy, and it becomes a self-fulfilling prophecy. He becomes what he thinks.

Your words are crucial in building up their inner strength so that when they encounter obstacles, they hear your voice of encouragement and words of wisdom. When they hear you say that you believe in them and they can accomplish anything, it allows them to go further towards their dreams and goals. Your voice becomes their internal voice and replaces the fear and doubt that arise during challenging times.

Teens need to know their strengths and develop their talents. They need to hear the positive voices of adults, whether it be parents, guardians, teachers, or mentors. Knowing their capabilities not only allows them to move through the challenge quicker but also catapults them far above it, so they achieve more than they ever imagined.

CHAPTER 10 - APOLOGIES MAKE A DIFFERENCE

I saw a video of a mom on social media who accused her kids of taking her phone charger. She went on a long rant about it. A few minutes later, she found her charger in her purse but didn't apologize. She merely said, 'If you didn't take my things all of the time, I wouldn't have thought you took my charger." Then after a few seconds, she said, "Do you want to get some ice cream?" Getting ice cream was her way of apologizing. But kids need to hear the actual words "I'm sorry," just like you do.

Over the years, the one thing I've noticed is that many parents have difficulty admitting when they are wrong. They have a hard time apologizing to their teens.

There may be times when you misinterpret your teens' actions. You may blame them for something they didn't do. You may say things in the heat of an argument that is belittling and that you regret saying.

Apologies are important because they teach your teens that being wrong is okay. It shows them that parents can make mistakes and that it's okay to own up to it and apologize for it. They respect you for that and recognize that you value them as individuals.

When you blame your kids falsely, treat them poorly, or overreact, they internalize those hurtful feelings. It's essential to clear the air in the present moment to prevent resentment from spilling over into future interactions. When you authentically apologize, the negative energy between you and your teens disappears.

Apologizing is not a sign of weakness. It shows strength by displaying that you are comfortable with who you are. It demonstrates that you are not afraid to admit when you have made a mistake. It teaches your children how to have effective interactions with people and shows them that making mistakes is part of being human.

CHAPTER 11 - EXPRESSING YOUR LOVE

Another key to reducing conflict is to make sure your teens know that they're loved. One day a mom brought her 15-year-old daughter to see me. She thought the girl was overweight and wanted her to go on a diet. She constantly told her daughter to lose weight and commented on her eating habits. Their relationship became strained. Her daughter did not appreciate her mother's constant badgering. They became distant and argued all the time.

The teen was indeed overweight, but after talking to her, it was clear that she had extremely low self-esteem. Her reduced self-confidence was due in part to her weight. But it also stemmed from thinking that her mother did not love and accept her the way she was. She didn't understand that her mother wanted her to be healthy and that her mother's continued focus on her weight was an effort to move her into action.

Most parents want their children to be healthy, happy, and successful. This desire can put undue pressure on teens. They think your love is tied to their performance. Your expectations may be high, but they need to be reassured that you will continue to love them no matter the outcome.

Acknowledging your teens is essential. It's easy to praise good grades or obtaining a lead role in the school play. But it's important to recognize the little, daily successes that occur along the way. It demonstrates that you embrace and accept them for who they are and what they are doing right now. It fosters confidence and reduces their self-doubt.

We all have a story, a journey that has brought us this far. Don't be afraid to share it. Share your ups as well as downs, not as a lecture but as part of a conversation. As you share about your challenges, you open up space for your teens to share their challenges. Telling your story is educational, will spark a conversation, and create a connection. The point of sharing is not to make them feel guilty by showing them how much harder your life was as a child. The purpose is to reveal that you, too, are human. It demonstrates that experiencing challenges and obstacles is a normal part of life.

Teens are smart. They know what's happening around them. They realize when there is tension in the marriage. They recognize when you are struggling to make ends meet. They discern when you are happy and when you are upset. They hear you crying in the other room. They see you celebrating when you get a promotion. You may not think they watch you, but they do.

Being vulnerable creates connection. It's okay to share about your failures and embarrassing moments as well as your successes. Your teens need to see how you handle all aspects of life. If they see you surmount obstacles, they know that they can do the same. They will have real examples to refer to when life gets complicated.

You can foster this connection by making sure you spend one-on-one time with your teens daily. Even fifteen minutes of quality time will help cultivate your relationship. Make sure this time is headphone-free.

Most people try to avoid silence by filling it with meaningless chatter or by listening to music. Honor the silences. A long pause in the conversation may seem awkward and may make you uncomfortable. But silence is an essential part of generating conversation.

When things are quiet, your teens may start to talk about an upsetting situation at school. Silence facilitates an opening for new conversations. These discussions may not arise amid constant chatter or background noise. Treasure it and use it to your advantage.

Some parents avoid outwardly expressing affection and think their actions speak louder than words. But teens must hear you say three words, "I love you." It might not be easy for you to say out loud. Practice in the mirror if you have to. Hearing those three words and knowing that you care for them is crucial. It creates a safe space between the two of you.

You may disagree with their actions. You may have to ground them for breaking your rules or being out of line. Even so, they will be more willing to talk to you about their upsets, challenges, and mistakes. They will come to you because they know that your love is constant.

CHAPTER 12 - LEARN HOW TO LISTEN

Listening is Key

Listening is critical to maintaining a solid connection with your teens. It reduces conflict and creates closer relationships. Listening is one of the most important skills we use throughout our lives. Unless you are trained in communication or counseling, most people never are formally taught how to listen. We just listen and think we are doing it well.

Have your teens ever accused you of not listening? Have you ever nodded your head during a conversation and pretended to listen as you thought about your plans for the day? Often we say we are listening, but we are not.

We may hear our teens' words but aren't fully paying attention to what they are saying. As they're talking, we are often thinking of how to respond or fix things.

Your daughter, for example, may be talking about a problem she is having with a friend. When she is speaking, you may find yourself thinking about the solution. You end up filtering out parts of the conversation as you listen for an opening to speak and give your opinion. We all do this. It's human nature.

Our listening is also clouded by our perceptions of people as well as our past experiences. If I ask you to describe a "teen" for me, there are adjectives that immediately pop into your mind. What are they? Your description may include words like rebellious, argumentative, adventurous, know-it-alls, self-absorbed, and challenging. Or you may say they're bold, passionate, and curious.

How you choose to describe teenagers depends upon your perception of them. It may not be the truth. It's not who they are. It's your perception of who they are. It's the colored glasses through which you see them and the filter through which you hear them.

If you think your son is argumentative, you listen to him through that filter. Before he even starts to talk, your guard is up. You are ready for him to challenge or question your viewpoint. When he begins to speak, you may not fully listen because you think you already know what he will say. You only hear snippets of the conversation because you're waiting to respond. He senses this, so when he accuses you of not listening, he's probably right.

Listen Without Judgement and Interruption
It's essential to listen to your teens without interrupting or judging what they're saying. It's so easy to jump in and tell teens what they should or should not do. It's natural to give them solutions, but sometimes all they want to do is talk, cry, vent, or tell you how they feel.

I know this is hard, and it's difficult to stay quiet. Even now, when my daughter talks to me, I occasionally slip. I interrupt the flow of the conversation to insert my opinion. She may be talking about an issue with a friend or about her job search. As soon as I interrupt to say, "Why don't you…?" she curtly says, "Never mind. You're not listening," and stops the conversation.

Your teenagers don't necessarily want your opinion. They don't always want you to fix things. They just want to talk. They want you to listen. As they talk, they often come to their own conclusions and figure things out for themselves.

It may be beneficial to ask your teens how they would like you to listen. Do they want your opinion, or do they want to vent? Knowing this upfront will guide your responses. It will make you a more effective listener.

Listen for Their Greatness
The context from which you listen is critical. Many teens with Attention Deficit Hyperactivity Disorder (ADHD) have trouble in school. It takes them longer to get their work done, and they have to study a lot harder to do well in their classes. Some kids with ADHD think they're dumb because they can't grasp the material as quickly as their classmates. As their parent, you know they're not dumb. You know their true potential and can see past those negative labels they attach to themselves. It's your role to advocate for the person you know them to be.

Some kids get into trouble at school. They may skip school or break the rules in other ways. Their actions are also not indicative of who they are. Their teachers may categorize them as problem students, which is a label that could stick with them for the rest of their lives. They often get pushed to the side, and their talent is overlooked and underdeveloped.

Your job as a parent is to recognize and cultivate the true spirit and passion of your teens. They need to know and feel that their future is full of possibilities. Listen for their potential. Listen for their greatness. Your task is to find their passions and develop their talents. It's essential to encourage them, so they can thrive and contribute their gifts to the world.

CHAPTER 13 - BE INTERESTED AND ENGAGED

It's critical to take an interest in what your teens like to do. Showing interest will increase the connection between the two of you. Understanding what teens think or how they feel starts with learning who they are.

If your daughter loves watching anime and you hate it, watch it with her anyway. If your son likes hip hop and you don't, listen to it at least part of the time in the car ride to school. You can learn a lot about your teens when you ask them questions about the activities they enjoy.

When your kids see that you are interested in what they are doing, they get excited. It's a big deal for them, even if they don't admit it. Their musical taste may be light years away from yours but listen to a few songs with them before switching the station. Being interested shows that you value them and indirectly says that you care.

My daughter has always loved to listen to electronic dance music. I grew up on R&B and rock, so I am not sure how or why she started listening to EDM. At first, her music sounded like a combination of discordant sounds, but I let her listen to it in the car as we drove to her various activities.

When she wanted to learn how to create it, my husband and I enrolled her in music production classes. We escorted her to music festivals, using earplugs to protect our ears from the deafening sounds coming from the DJs on stage. We shook our heads in amazement as we watched kids jump up and down in huge crowds in front of the stage. I didn't like the music at first, but with time it grew on me, and now I choose to listen to it even when I'm by myself. Lauryn's interest in EDM has now become one of her passions. As a young adult, she has developed a musical brand and produces her own music.

One way to discover more about your teens is by interviewing them. Their insights and perspectives on life may surprise you. Schedule a time to sit down with them for at least 30 minutes and ask them questions. Here are some to get you started.

1. What do you love about your life?

2. What do you hate about your life?

3. What can you count on me for?

4. What can't you count on me for?

5. What do I do that annoys you the most?

6. What do I do that you like?

7. How can I be most helpful?

When your teens start to respond, try not to interrupt or comment. Your job is to listen and learn more about their point of view.

Another way to connect with your teens is to be engaged in their lives. Teachers, school administrators, instructors, coaches, and other adults are responsible for many kids. You are the one who is fully invested in your teens' best interest.

It's important to advocate for your adolescents. But keep in mind that your role is to guide them, not manage every aspect of their lives. You have to check yourself along the way to make sure you're not becoming too enmeshed. You don't want to cross the line and become that helicopter parent.

Get to know their teachers, their coaches, and their friends. Knowing their inner circle of friends is essential. You get a sense of who they hang out with and what types of activities they enjoy. You prove to your kids that you are interested in them and care about what they do. Their friends also know that you are a person they can trust, and you become a part of their network as well.

Being engaged in school activities is also important. It lets the teachers and coaches know who you are and what you stand for. If you have a working relationship with them, they can often give you a heads up when something goes awry. It's also important to be involved in parent organizations. You'll gain insight into how things work within the school and are more aware of available resources.

Being engaged may be very difficult for working parents, especially those who may work two or three jobs. But I suggest choosing a family member or friend to stand in for you if you don't have the time. If you can't go to a game, perhaps someone else can be there to cheer for your teen. If you can't go to a recital or back to school night, perhaps your relative can go in your place. Being supportive and available are key ingredients in creating closer relationships. But you don't have to do it alone. It's essential to build a support network around you.

CHAPTER 14 - ASK FOR HELP

It's imperative to ask for help. You may think you are the only one feeling distraught, overwhelmed, and inadequate. But if you talk and share with others, you will find many in the same boat. Thinking you're the only one increases your stress and anxiety. You're not alone. Many parents feel embarrassed and guilty because they don't know what to do. It's trial and error most of the time.

It's essential to create a support network. You need people to share your triumphs and your failures, and believe me; you will have both. Join parenting groups, read books, watch videos, or talk to counselors and therapists. Seeking help is not a weakness. It shows that you are doing all you can to be the best parent you can be.

Be aware that teens may experience anxiety, depression, and other mental health issues. These are beyond your control, and you need the help of health care professionals. Some of the red flags for mental illness may involve subtle changes in communication. You can recognize these changes if you have had ongoing, open conversations with them. This is why it's so important to strengthen your connection with your teens.

Red flags include:[21]

- Depressed mood
- Significant changes in weight or sleep patterns
- Decreased participation and interest in activities
- Expressions of hopelessness
- Self-mutilation or mentioning that they want to hurt themselves
- Increased social isolation
- Change in tone of their voice (for example, they are always somber when they used to be upbeat)
- Change in responses (for example, they respond with "I don't know" and "leave me alone" more than usual)
- Change in communication pattern (for example, they stop texting or avoid eye contact)

If you have any concerns about your teen's mental health, contact your pediatrician or family physician right away. Your adolescent may need to see a therapist or a psychiatrist. Therapy and medication are not signs of weakness or an indication of your inadequacy as a parent. It shows that you are providing your child with resources to be successful. Refer to the Appendix for additional support in the area of mental health.

Mentors are another essential part of your teens' support system because they can guide them in areas beyond your expertise. If your daughter is good at science, her physician or science teacher can answer questions about that career pathway or suggest courses to take. If your son is a dancer, the dance instructor or a more advanced student can help guide him.

Most teens don't listen to their parents. When I talk to teens, I frequently offer the same advice as their parents, but they listen to me for two reasons. I'm an expert, but most importantly, I'm not their parent. Teens frequently tune their parents out and tend to do the opposite of what they want them to do. That's why it's essential to have people you can trust and rely on to reinforce your message and values.

Your teens need a safety net around them to catch them when they fall and guide them through tough times. Having a trusted village is vital. You may not always be able to provide them with what they need, but someone in your community will.

CHAPTER 15 - PARENTING THROUGH THE PANDEMIC

The pandemic has put a whole new spin on parenting. It's created worry, strain, and tension on parents and teens. Many of you have been working from home while simultaneously managing your children's remote learning. If you are an essential worker, you have been going to work despite the higher risk of exposure to Covid-19. You might also be dealing with the loss of loved ones and job security.

You've been isolated from family and friends, and there haven't been many outlets outside the home. Even though the availability of vaccines will allow people to move around more freely, you may have many lingering questions and concerns.

You might be wondering about the long-term impact of remote learning on the overall education of your children. Is your teens' education from home as robust and effective as if they were in school? Will they be on par with other kids their age when they go back to school? What's the effect on their social and emotional development?

Teens have lost the ability to hang out with their peers and participate in extracurricular activities. They are stuck at home with their family and don't have many places to go, especially if they can't drive. Many milestone events have been canceled, like sweet sixteen parties, proms, graduations, and competitions. College students struggle with asserting their independence while taking classes from home, and they miss being with their friends. Everyone's trying to adapt and manage their different lives under the same roof, and it's exhausting. We are all going through a grieving process. The first thing you can do to help your teens is to permit them to feel.

In her book *On Death and Dying,* Dr. Elisabeth Kübler-Ross developed five stages of grief as a bereavement model. [22] Although several alternative models have been proposed since then, I think these five stages are the best way to understand what we all have experienced during this challenging period. I am going to walk you through these stages from your adolescents' perspective, but feel free to use this model to understand your response to the pandemic as well.

- The first stage is denial. Your teens initially may have been in a state of shock as their life instantaneously changed. One minute they were in school with their friends, and the next minute they were isolated at home, learning remotely. In this stage, it was natural for them to feel numb and question the validity of what was happening around them. Your teens might have thought that there was no way that the situation was real. Denial is an important defense mechanism to avoid being overwhelmed with the situation.

- Anger is the second stage and is necessary to get to the other side. In this stage, it's natural for your teens to say things like "Why me?" or "Life's not fair." They may take their anger out on close friends and family. Your teens need to express their anger. The more they resist those feelings, the more they persist.

- The third stage is bargaining. It's the "should have, would have, could have, if only" phase. Your teens might be thinking about all the activities that they missed because schools have been closed. Your college students, especially seniors, might regret not having had enough time to spend with their friends.

- Depression or sadness is the fourth stage that your adolescents may experience. They will be sad, teary-eyed, and emotional at times. Some teens may not want to talk and would prefer to be alone. All these feelings are natural and expected since their lives have been upended.

- Acceptance is the final and last stage of grief, according to Elizabeth Kübler-Ross's model; it's when your teens realize that life will go on. They come to terms with their "new" reality of remote learning, wearing facemasks, and social distancing. It's a time when they accept and adjust to this new way of life.

It's essential to allow your teens to go through the grieving process. They have to get to the stage of acceptance before they can move forward. Suppressing their feelings will only prolong their emotional suffering and affect their ability to effectively deal with this challenging life event.

Don't let the circumstances define who they are. Let who they are and what they want to accomplish in life determine how they respond to the circumstances. Acknowledging their feelings and supporting them as they move through the grieving process is crucial. Be kind to yourself. Be sure to give your teens and yourself space and grace as you move forward and deal with the impact of the pandemic on your lives.

CHAPTER 16 - SELF-CARE IS CRUCIAL

Its Importance
Self-care is critical for parents, but it's often low on the priority list. You're busy taking your kids to activities and making sure they do their homework. You are balancing work and home life. By the time your day ends, you may be exhausted and have no time to do anything else but sleep.

Deferring your physical and emotional needs will lead to physical and mental burnout. It will also lead to increased conflict with your teens. Eating junk food between meetings and activities may satisfy your appetite momentarily, but it doesn't provide the long-term nutrients for your body to function effectively. Your abrupt changes in sugar levels cause mood swings and impatience. Your fatigue leads to frustration, stress, and meltdowns.

It's essential to look after your well-being because if you don't, no one else will. If you are not well, the entire family will not be well. Your actions impact the "state of the family."

Mindfulness

Developing a few daily practices that will promote good physical and mental health is essential. You don't have to run three miles or go to the gym every day. Mindfulness meditation exercises are simple and easy to do. They can include breathing exercises, meditations with mantras, and yoga. As demonstrated in Chapter 5, you can take as little as ten minutes to get yourself centered and stay in the present moment.

Mindfulness can help provide greater empathy and compassion. It improves your attention and positively impacts your interactions. It enables you to cope better by increasing your resilience.

Studies have shown that mindfulness increases the neuroplasticity of the brain. In other words, the brain reorganizes and rewires itself. It forms new neural connections that boost your levels of peace and happiness by shifting connections in areas of the brain responsible for emotions, including the hippocampus and amygdala.[23]

Mindfulness exercises that focus on breathing are simple ways to center yourself. We ordinarily don't think about breathing because it's automatic. It's something that we just do. But when you focus on each breath, a funny thing happens. Your mind begins to clear itself of all other thoughts. It's too hard for your mind to think about anything other than breathing.

When you feel yourself getting stressed, focus on your breath. As you do this, thoughts may come and go. Let them float by as if they're clouds in the sky. Don't hang on to them. Notice them and let them keep floating away. As you practice, you can increase the time and incorporate other meditation and mindfulness practices listed in the Appendix.

Me-time

Me-time is important. It means spending time doing something for yourself. You don't have to take a lot of time. It can just be 15 minutes a day, but it's crucial to schedule time to replenish yourself. You could spend me-time reading a book, meditating, going to the salon, taking a long bath, playing tennis, or enjoying a cup of coffee on your patio. Me-time also includes nurturing meaningful relationships by scheduling outings with your spouse, significant other, or friends.

Taking time out for yourself is not selfish. You have to recharge to be able to attend to the needs of everyone else. Self-care is essential to maintaining your vitality and peace of mind. You will find that you are less reactive and more thoughtful in challenging situations. Caring for yourself is not a luxury. It's essential to your well-being and the well-being of the entire family.

CHAPTER 17 - PUTTING IT ALL TOGETHER

Conflicts during the teenage years are inevitable. Adolescent years are fraught with tension, self-doubt, stress, and worry, but they can also be a time of engaging conversation, mentoring, and contribution. You can strengthen your relationship, and you and your teens can still be close.

Remind yourself that your teens are growing up in a different world and that you have distinct points of view. They have their own personalities and aren't miniature versions of you. Remember not to take things personally and focus on nurturing your relationships by expressing your love, being interested, and being engaged.

You can reduce the conflict with your teens by shifting how you communicate. Listen more. Speak less. Acknowledge and validate their perspectives. Enjoy being with them in the present moment, and remember that the future is never promised.

Older generations have called Generation Z "snowflakes." They say they lack resilience and fortitude. Gen Z is far from being a generation of snowflakes. Your teens are strong, determined, and persistent individuals. They want to make this world a better place, and you now have the skills to help them do that.

Teens have endless potential, but they need to know that you care and that they matter. They want to be heard, understood, and appreciated for the contributions they can make now.

Listen for their greatness. Resolve your disagreements, and empower your teens to let their light shine for all the world to see.

Now that you know how to reduce conflict and connect with your teens, the next step is to take action. For guidance on putting the concepts of this book into practice, go to www.boostyourconnectionwithyourteen.com to register for my *21 Day Boost Your Connection with Your Teen E-mail Challenge Course*.

The Next Step

If you haven't done so already, I encourage you to take advantage of my Bonus gift that I mentioned at the beginning of this book. I'd like to give you exclusive access to my audio training, "The Extraterrestrial Approach To Listening."

Go to www.youarenotabadparent.com to access your bonus gift.

For step-by-step guidance on putting the concepts of this book into practice, go to my website
www.boostyourconnectionwithyourteen.com.

About The Author

Dr. Elizabeth R. Henry (Dr. Liz) is a board-certified pediatrician, parent coach, speaker, author, and workshop facilitator with over 20 years of experience. She is a trusted advisor to parents and youth and the founder of Dr. Liz Consulting.

Through her virtual coaching sessions, webinars and courses, she provides parents with tools and resources to connect, communicate, and support their preteens, teens, and young adults.

She has created and delivered student workshops for numerous organizations, including Princeton University, Kean University, the University of Southern California, Raritan Valley Community College, the Congressional Caucus on Black Women and Girls, and the Girl Scouts. She has also served as a medical expert for corporations.

She graduated from Princeton University and the University of Pennsylvania's Perelman School of Medicine. She completed her pediatric residency at Georgetown University Hospital in Washington, D.C., then subsequently worked at the Children's Hospital of Philadelphia before joining a private practice in New Jersey.

Dr. Liz is a fellow of the American Academy of Pediatrics and a member of the American Medical Association, New Jersey Medical Society, and Middlesex County Medical Society. She has been honored for her work with youth by several associations and publications, including the Girl Scouts, Boy Scouts, NAACP, and Alpha Kappa Alpha Sorority, Inc. She was also named Healthcare Hero and one of the Top 50 Women in Business by NJBIZ.

Dr. Liz has appeared as a guest on numerous television and radio shows, as well as podcasts. She is an expert for YourTango.com, a leading online magazine.

She is a lifetime Girl Scout, member of Alpha Kappa Sorority, Inc., The National Drifters, Inc., and a past board member of the Raritan Valley Community College Foundation. She is married and has a daughter in her twenties.

APPENDIX

Meditation/Self Care Apps

1. Headspace
2. Calm
3. Relax Melodies
4. Shine
5. Art of Living Journey
6. Insight Timer
7. Sattva
8. Smiling Mind
9. Ten Percent Happier
10. Reflectly

Mental Health Resources

For those seeking a therapist or on-line counseling:

www.theravive.com

www.goodtherapy.com

www.betterhelp.com (Online Counseling)

www.therapytribe.com

www.christiancounselordirectory.com

www.therapyforblackgirls.com

www.therapyforblackmen.org

www.ethniccounselors.com

www.blacktherapistsrock.com

www.muslimmentalhealth.com

www.lgbtqtherapistresource.com

www.nqttcn.com/directory (National Queer and Trans Therapist of Color)

www.talktoivy.com (Online Counseling)

www.talkspace.com (Online counseling)

For those seeking free or low-cost counseling services:

www.opencounseling.com

www.ccdom.org (Catholic Charities)

National Suicide Prevention Lifeline: 1-800-273-8255

General Resources for Parents:

Jensen, France E with Amy Ellis Nutt. *The Teenage Brain: A Neuroscientist's Survival Guide to Raising Adolescents and Young Adults.* New York: HarperCollins Publishers, 2015.

American Academy of Pediatrics website — www.healthychildren.org

You can find a host of other resources on my website — www.drlizconsulting.com

NOTES

[1] Dimock, Michael. "Defining Generations: Where Millennials end and Generation Z begins." *pewresearch.org*. Pew Research Center, 17 Jan 2019. https://www.pewresearch.org/fact-tank/2019/01/17/where-millennials-end-and-generation-z-begins/

[2] Ryback, Ralph. "From Baby Boomers to Generation Z." *psychologytoday.org*. Psychology Today, 22 Feb 2016. https://www.psychologytoday.com/us/blog/the-truisms-wellness/201602/baby-boomers-generation-z

[3] Dimock, Michael. "Defining Generations: Where Millennials end and Generation Z begins." *pewresearch.org*.

[4] Ryback, Ralph. "From Baby Boomers to Generation Z." *psychologytoday.org*.

[5] Dimock, Michael. "Defining Generations: Where Millennials end and Generation Z begins." *pewresearch.org*.

[6] Ryback, Ralph. "From Baby Boomers to Generation Z." *psychologytoday.org*.

[7] Dimock, Michael. "Defining Generations: Where Millennials end and Generation Z begins." *pewresearch.org*.

[8] Parker, Kim, Nikki Graff, and Ruth Igielnik. "Generation Z Looks a Lot Like Millennials on Key Social and Political Issues." *pewresearch.org*. Pew Research Center, 19 Jan 2021. https://www.pewresearch.org/social-trends/2019/01/17/generation-z-looks-a-lot-like-millennials-on-key-social-and-political-issues/

[9] Diekema, Douglas S. "Adolescent Brain Development and Medical Decision Making." *pediatrics.aappublications.org*. Pediatrics, August 2020, 146 (Supplement 1) S18-S24. https://pediatrics.aappublications.org/content/146/Supplement_1/S18

[10] Jensen, France E with Amy Ellis Nutt. *The Teenage Brain: A Neuroscientist's Survival Guide to Raising Adoescents and Young Adults*. New York: HarperCollins Publishers, 2015. Print.

[11] Chua, Amy. *The Battle Hymn of the Tiger Mother*. New York: Penguin Books, 2011. Digital.

[12] Wang, Yanan "Tragedy of 'golden' daughter's fall resonates with Asian immigrant children." *The Washington Post,* 27 July 2015. Digital. https://www.washingtonpost.com/news/morning-mix/wp/2015/07/27/tragedy-of-golden-daughters-murder-plot-against-parents-resonates-with-asian-immigrant-children/

[13] "Understanding the stress response." *health.harvard.edu.* Harvard Health Publishing, 6 Jul 2020 (updated). March 2011 (published).

[14] "Understanding the stress response." *health.harvard.edu.*

[15] "Understanding the stress response." *health.harvard.edu.*

[16] "How stress affects your health." *apa.org.* American Psychological Association, 1 Nov. 2018. https://www.apa.org/topics/stress/body

[17] "Chronic stress puts your health at risk." *mayoclinic.org.* Mayo Clinic, 19 Mar. 2019. https://www.mayoclinic.org/healthy-lifestyle/stress-management/in-depth/stress/art-20046037

[18] Henry, Elizabeth, host. "An International Discussion on Parenting." *Ten Going on Twenty – Parenting Preteens to Young Adults with Dr. Liz,* season 1, episode 5, Podbean. 22 Nov. 2020. https://drlizconsulting.podbean.com/e/health-and-happiness-for-parents-an-international-perspective/

[19] Taylor, John A. *Notes from an Unhurried Journey.* Fall Walls Eight Windows, New York: 1991. Print.

[20] Henry, Elizabeth, host. "We are Not Snowflakes." *Ten Going on Twenty - Parenting Preteens to Young Adults with Dr. Liz,* season 1, episode 3, Podbean, 22 May 2020. https://drlizconsulting.podbean.com/e/we-are-not-snowflakes/

[21] *Diagnostic and Statistical Manual of Mental Disorders (DSM-V).* American Psychiatric Publishing, 5th ed. Washington, DC. 2013. Print

[22] Kubler-Ross, Elizabeth. *On Death & Dying.* New York: Scribner, 2014. Digital

[23] Riopel, Leslie. "Mindfulness and the Brain: What Does Research and Neuroscience Say." *positive psychology.com.* Positive Psychology, 11 Sept 2020. Web. 25 Oct 2020. https://positivepsychology.com/mindfulness-brain-research-neuroscience/

Made in the USA
Monee, IL
23 July 2021